DENVER & SURROUNDINGS
10 Locals Tell You Where to Go, What to Eat, & How to Fit In

ISBN-13: 978-1535586399

CONTENTS

ABOUT THIS BOOK

This book is for people who want to see another side of Colorado.

To explore the main attractions, certainly, but also find the hidden-away trail that most visitors overlook. To discover that Colorado is home to not only mountains, but a desert full of sand dunes. To find the best cheesesteaks this side of Philly. And to learn where locals hang out

In other words, this book is for people who want to get under the skin of a new place. Who want to rent apartments and live in local neighborhoods. Who want to eat in tiny restaurants full of locals in the know. Who want to deepen their experience of this wild, beautiful part of the United States.

Think of this as a supplement to your traditional guidebooks. Use those for their handy place histories, lists of local hotels (if that's your style), and restaurant pricing charts. And then use this to go deeper—to figure out how to find the most interesting neighborhoods, the most delicious restaurants, and that hidden-away hiking trail just outside the city.

Getting excited? Me too. (Just wait till you read some of these interviews!)

Now, a little orientation:

This book is split into 10 interviews with people who live in Denver, Colorado Springs, Boulder, and the areas around those major cities. Many have lived in their cities and towns for decades. Some were born and raised in the region. And all of them love showing travelers the best their place has to offer.

Throughout the book, below each person's name, you'll see a short bio designed to help you understand his or her background. If you are passionate about food, look for someone whose short bio includes "foodie" or "chef." If you're a culture lover, look for a culture lover. And so on and so forth.

ABOUT THIS BOOK

Some of the interviewees are also tour guides, artists, business owners, or bloggers. Watch for web addresses under their interviews if you'd like to learn more about their art, blogs, tours, or businesses.

Now, then, into the book...

ON TRAVELING LIKE A LOCAL

Like many well-touristed places, Colorado has two faces.

There's the face that most tourists see, full of busy shopping streets, crowded viewpoints, and well-known monuments and attractions—like Coor's Field and Denver's 16th Street Mall.

Some of these things are worth seeing and experiencing (as my interviewees will tell you); they're famous for a reason.

BUT.

They aren't the whole story of Denver and its surroundings.

There's another face, another story—one that the locals live every day—full of up-and-coming wine bars, less-trafficked hiking trails, and weekend ski runs.

For me, the goal of any travel is to experience this other side of an area, to slip into the culture, to try to understand it, to feel—even if I am only there for a few days—like I am truly living in that place, experiencing it like a local would.

I'm sure many of you feel the same.

Which is, of course, the whole point of this book.

In over 16 years of short-term international trips and nearly four years of traveling full-time, I've come up with a routine that makes me feel more like a local. And the most important thing I've found is simply this: **the best way to live like a local is to ask locals.**

Which is why, for those of us who don't have a local friend to show us around, I've collected these interviews and written this book.

Before you dive into the interviews, though, here are five more ways to experience Colorado (or any place, really) in a fresh, authentic, local-centric way:

ON TRAVELING LIKE A LOCAL

1. Travel slowly. Spend some real time in a place. The only way to see all of a city's hidden corners is to spend time exploring it.

2. Rent apartments, preferably in a neighborhood full of local people. (Not sure how to find the right neighborhood? I've asked locals to tell us in the interviews you'll find in this book. Not sure how to find apartments? My personal starting point is Airbnb: *airbnb.com/c/ggriffis*.)

3. Shop at fresh markets, small butcher shops, and neighborhood bakeries. This is where you'll find the best food (as opposed to the grocery store).

4. Make friends with people who live there. Ask people about their lives, their thoughts, and their backgrounds. Expats and locals are both incredibly fascinating, and every conversation will teach you a lot.

5. Try to fit in. In Colorado, this means don't smoke, do respect the cyclists, and dress casual.

It is these principles and this type of travel that I've molded the questions in this book around. So, if you, too, want to slow down and experience Colorado in a different way, these interviews are for you.

THE INTERVIEWS

DENVER
Colorado's capitol city & gateway to the Rockies.

FIND WI-FI HERE: Union Station, Black Eye Coffee in Capitol Hill, Denver Bicycle Café, Carbon Beverage Café, & Starbucks.

Dominic & Sarah Arnone
Hikers. Art-Lovers. Skiers. Microbrewery Fans.

About Dominic & Sarah

Dominic: I'm a native New Yorker who's lived in Denver for the past six years. I work for the local utility, Xcel Energy, as an electrical engineer designing substations. In my free time, I explore this great state of ours and the Tennyson Street Art District a few blocks from my house. There's a thriving scene of entrepreneurs building some beautiful businesses in this area.

Sarah: I'm a Colorado native, born and raised in Golden five minutes from the Coors Brewery, which was founded in 1873. I am currently working as a Medical Assistant at a family practice. In my free time, I enjoy hiking, skiing or tubing in the winter, and drinking an unending supply of microbrews from the 60+ breweries in the Denver Metro area.

What to do in Denver (the Basics)

Start with a visit to Union Station—a converted train station, which is still a transportation hub, actually, but now also a hotel and nine restaurants/bars. It also has a large common area with comfortable seating and a few shuffleboard tables.

The Denver Museum of Nature and Science and Denver Zoo are in the same general area in Denver's City Park and are both worth a visit.

THE INTERVIEWS

The Coors Brewery in Golden is fun if you have time for a trip west of town. It can be really really busy on the weekends, so try to go on a weekday. There's a guided/self-guided tour (depending on day and how busy they are) and you get three free beers.

Water World, 20 minutes north of downtown, is one of America's largest outdoor water parks.

And the Red Rocks Amphitheater, 20 minutes west of downtown, is a world-class music venue set in a large natural outdoor amphitheatre.

As for things that are not worth seeing? Six Flags Elitch Gardens, Denver Aquarium, and the famous dinner + show venue Casa Bonita (unless you eat beforehand and don't mind paying for food you won't and *shouldn't* eat).

Hidden Gems for Seasoned Travelers
Microbreweries are a lot of fun and there are a ton of them here. And we're fans of the Denver Botanic Gardens, which are a well-cared-for little oasis in the middle of the city and not on many people's radar, so you can have some space to yourself.

Where to Stay
We like Capitol Hill and the Highlands. Both are very close to downtown, with good access to public transport, but outside the main downtown core. Capitol Hill feels a little rougher, but is very interesting and fun. The Highlands is a bit more polished.

Day Trips
Boulder is well worth the trip if you love good hiking and shopping and interesting people. Make sure to walk down Pearl Street while you're there. And keep in mind that driving there can be a pain (so park and walk as much as you can).

9

THE INTERVIEWS

We're also fans of Rocky Mountain National Park, which is very close, and Estes Park, up near the park and full of interesting shops, mountain culture, and beautiful wildlife. Pro tip: don't approach the elk.

Fort Collins is the place to go for breweries, including the famed Fat Tire.

The Garden of the Gods is beautiful and the sand dunes are something special—a bizarre, striking desert landscape in the middle of Colorado. Make sure when you go that you're ready for the thunderstorms that roll in in the afternoons. Go early. It's a once-in-a-lifetime thing.

Glenwood Springs, if you want to go that far (2.5 hours into the mountains), has a fun theme park on top of a mountain. Take the gondola to the top and ride the swing (which swings you off the top of the mountain) if you're adventurous. There are some great things for kids up there, too. But keep in mind that it's pay-per-ride.

Finally, head to Mount Evans, where you'll find the highest paved road in America leading to the very top of the mountain.

Where to Walk
Washington Park, City Park, the Cherry Creek Bike Path, and Platte River Greenway are all beautiful places for a stroll in the city.

What & Where to Eat & Drink
Must-trys include green chiles, Rocky Mountain oysters, and burgers and our favorite restaurants include:

The Populist (3163 Larimer Street; phone: 720.432.3163), which is a bit pricey but well worth it. It's got very interesting food and is in an up-and-coming area of the city. The jackfruit (made to taste like pork) was particularly delicious.

10

THE INTERVIEWS

Cuba Cuba (1173 Delaware Street; phone: 303.605.2822), a gorgeous renovated house in the middle of the city. It's out of place, but beautiful, full of vibrant colors. It feels like a bit of Cuba in the middle of Denver. They don't take reservations, so you'll usually end up waiting, but don't worry: mojitos are available while you wait. We really like the tostones, grilled plantains with garlic mojo.

Linger (2030 W. 30th Avenue; phone: 303.993.3120), which is so weird it's hard to talk about. I mean, how do you describe a mortuary converted to a restaurant that they've somehow made cool and fun and not gross, so don't worry? This is one of four active restaurants from one of the city's best restauranteurs, Justin Cucchi.

Freshcraft (1530 Blake street, Suite A; phone: 303.758.9608), which is always one of the better spots for sampling beers (large brew menus are abundant around town, but they've got one of the best). The food is also a notch above the rest. Most breweries have a food truck outside or work with a nearby restaurant, but Freshcraft makes their own food. We recommend the steak frites.

Denver Ted's Cheesesteaks (1308 Pearl Street), which is run by a couple of stoners who make the best cheesesteak this side of Philly.

Budget Tips
Brothers Bar & Grill (1920 Market Street) has cheap drinks if you are looking to go out one night. And the 16th Street Mall has some cheaper options, though most are chain places (Chipotle, Subway, Corner Bakery).

How to Fit In
Smoking is strange here. Coloradans don't really do it. Also, be nice. This is a nice place.

How to Meet Locals & Make Friends
Head to the breweries and strike up a conversation.

11

THE INTERVIEWS

Best Places to Take a Photo

Check out Union Station, Civic Center Park (the capitol buildings), the blue bear statue at the Convention Center, or City Park (in front of pond with the city as a backdrop). That last one is a pretty iconic Denver view.

Final Notes & Other Tips

Pot is legal here. But that doesn't mean there aren't rules. If you are going to indulge, know the laws. Don't overindulge. And don't try to take it home. (Seriously...don't try to take it home. Surrounding states aren't enthusiastic about the law and have set up checkpoints specifically for marijuana searches.)

Also, keep in mind that you are a mile above sea level...and that's just downtown. Make sure you drink *lots* of water while you're here. If you are planning on going to the mountains, it's wise to give yourself a day or two to acclimate to the altitude.

THE INTERVIEWS

Gigi Griffis
Hiker. Food Snob. Writer. Full-Time Traveler.

About Gigi

Hey there, friends. It's Gigi—the author of this little Colorado guidebook. Nice to meet you. When I'm not writing guide-books (or articles or websites), I spend as much time as I can outside. I love hiking, picnics, sleeping under the stars, and long-distance cycle trips. When I'm not outdoors, you'll usually find me reading, writing, cooking, chatting, traveling, or snug-gling my world-traveling pooch, Luna.

Before I started traveling full-time, I spent five years living in Denver—and I've been back quite a bit since—so here's my take on my former home, the mile-high city.

What to do in Denver (the Basics)

Start with a stroll through downtown. There are some beautiful streets (Larimer Square, in particular) and some interesting old industrial buildings now turned into ad agency offices and restaurants and breweries. Do some exploring and stop into the places that intrigue you most.

Next, for a taste of the cliché American west, make your way to The Stampede for some line dancing, cheap beers, a ride on the mechanical bull.

Finally, head to the Denver Zoo, especially if you have kids. It's a favorite of mine, particularly when there are new baby ani-mals to be seen. Weekdays are best for this, as weekends and free days get crowded fast.

Hidden Gems for Seasoned Travelers

For exceptionally good local music, check out the Under-ground Music Showcase (*theums.com*)—a summer festival held at a bunch of great little venues. Buy a wristband (ahead of time online), grab a schedule, and wander from venue to venue discovering new bands. It's where I found some of my own long-time favorites.

If you're not visiting during the UMS, there's probably still great music to be had (Denver has an excellent music scene). Try Swallow Hill for folk, bluegrass, and singer-songwriter stuff, Dazzle for jazz, and Soiled Dove Underground for a gorgeous variety of artists and genres.

Another gem is the Colorado Shakespeare Festival up in Boulder. Tickets are free and they do several plays each summer, mostly outdoors. They're always very well done and a pleasure to attend.

The Denver Chalk Art Festival is another fun one. It's held in Larimer Square in June and features some really stunning chalk art that doesn't look a thing like chalk.

Another June winner is the Capitol Hill People's Fair, which combines music and street food and lots of little art and food stands. This is the place to go if you're into handmade jewelry and hand-sewn dresses.

If you're here around Halloween, check out the Denver Zombie Crawl. Grab a spot on a patio and people-watch, camera in hand. Some of the costumes are amazing.

Finally, if you're a cyclist, Cherry Creek Bike Path is really lovely; you can ride all the way out to a pretty reservoir in Aurora.

Where to Stay
I love Washington Park for longer stays. It's a pretty neighborhood and a wonderful place to walk and there's a small lake with paddleboats and ducks. It's particularly breathtaking in the fall when the leaves are turning.

For shorter stays, downtown is probably the best option if you can afford it. You'll have easy access to the best food and entertainment there.

THE INTERVIEWS

Day Trips

My favorite ski town is Breckenridge. In the summer, it's a gorgeous mountain town full of hiking trails and cute boutique shops and a great little basement pizza place called Downstairs at Eric's (111 S. Main Street). In winter, you'll find snow and (of course) snow sports.

If you're into breweries, another great option is Golden, with its tiny microbreweries and pretty scenery.

If you've never been to a rodeo, Colorado has some great ones. Try to find something that fits your timeframe and make sure to watch the bull riding and mutton busting portions, which are wildly entertaining.

(Not familiar with mutton busting? It's where little kids don helmets and try to stay on the back of a sheep. If that sounds hilarious, it's because it is.)

And just outside town in Morrison, you'll find the Red Rocks Amphitheatre—a music venue carved into the rock. If you don't want to head out for a concert, just go up during the day and climb the steps for cool views.

Where to Walk

Cherry Creek State Park with its reservoir (dotted with sailboats in the summer) is my favorite spot for a walk. But it is a bit far from the center of town, so if you're looking for something closer, try Washington Park—a pretty park and small lake (full of paddle boats in summer) surrounded by a nice neighborhood full of pretty architecture.

What & Where to Eat & Drink

I have two all-time favorites in Denver. The first is Vesta Dipping Grill (1822 Blake Street; phone: 303.296.1970)—a restaurant where you order a simple entrée (steak, chicken, fish, or vegetarian) and choose three amazing homemade sauces to dip your meal in. This is my go-to spot for a nice night out.

THE INTERVIEWS

Tied for first place in my food-snob ranking is Bistro Vendome (1420 Larimer Street; phone: 303.825.3232), whose cracked pepper steak had me writing odes. I also love their fancy hamburgers and melt-in-your-mouth breakfast croissants with homemade jams.

I also absolutely adore Cru (1442 Larimer Street) for their wine flights and light fare. Theirs is the best tomato basil soup I've ever had—hands down. When you go, ask if you can eat on the back patio. Almost no one knows about it, so it's usually empty unless they're busy, and it's a quiet and cute place for a lunch or drink.

Then there's 9th Door (1808 Blake Street; phone: 303.292.2229)—a gorgeous Spanish tapas bar right next door to Vesta Dipping Grill. Try the fantastic artichokes and have a tinto de verano (half red wine, half orange soda) to drink.

Reservations are highly recommended if you're visiting any of the above places for dinner.

Finally, a couple honorable mentions:

For Italian-style pizza, check out Protos Pizza (2401 15th Street; phone: 720.855.9400).

My favorite hole-in-the-wall Chinese place is Healthy Asian Garden (284 S. Logan Street; phone: 303.722.7500).

Best Places to Take a Photo
Washington Park is quite pretty, as is the Cherry Creek Reservoir and, of course, the mountains. For downtown shots, check out Larimer Square (especially at Christmastime when it's all lit up) or the old warehouse buildings near Union Station.

Find Gigi at gigigriffis.com.

16

THE INTERVIEWS

Ruth Tobias
Freelance Food & Beverage Writer. Film Buff.

About Ruth
I'm a freelance food-and-beverage writer/editor and my signif-icant other is the artistic director of the Denver Film Society/ Denver Film Festival. So what we do in our free time is what we do for work: eat, drink, write, and watch movies.

I've been a Denverite for nine years.

What to do in Denver (the Basics)
Most of Denver's tourist attractions are worthwhile. We've got great museums, great pro sports, great outdoors activities (hiking, cycling, climbing, etc.), great and constant food, beer, and craft festivals, brewery tours, pot tourism—it's hard to go wrong! Even things that may not be of interest to me person-ally, like the US Mint, are apparently pretty edifying.

I'm a food writer, first and foremost, so three places that both visitors and locals love come to mind first: Union Station (our grand train station, also featuring a variety of restaurants), The Source (an artisan food market in an old 1980s brick foundry building), and Avanti F&B (a collective eatery).

Hidden Gems for Seasoned Travelers
Though it's temporarily closed to relocate, I adore the Kirkland Museum of Fine & Decorative Art. It's especially rich in Art Nou-veau and Art Deco pieces. Also, the Museum of Contem-porary Art is small but superb.

Where to Stay
If you're looking for a B&B or something in the hip neighbor-hoods with lots of shops/restaurants etc., the Highlands, Baker, and RiNo are the places to be. Keep in mind that RiNo is more edgy/artsy than upscale, though. It still looks pretty gritty.

THE INTERVIEWS

Day Trips

You can be in the mountains within 45 minutes, where you'll find a myriad of hiking areas. Towns like Evergreen and Nederland are fun cute little mountain towns and good stops en route to hiking or cycling trails. Evergreen also has a good natural skating rink in winter.

Breckenridge is about an hour and a half away and I like it because it's more rustic and colorful than many ski areas (like Vail and Aspen); it actually has a pre-ski history as a mining town, which is evident in the character of the old buildings along its many streets.

Boulder is about 30 minutes north and, besides being a college town, it's an old hippie enclave turned yuppie hub at the edge of the Flatirons. It's pretty and has a charming pedestrian mall full of great restaurants, lively bars, etc. And, of course, there's lots of hiking and cycling around the area.

Finally, an hour-plus south, there's a little art colony/Colorado Springs suburb called Manitou Springs that's charming.

What & Where to Eat & Drink

Colorado is more a place about ingredients than dishes—lamb, trout, bison, in the summer terrific local peaches and corn. That said, green chile is a *must* (it's different here than it is in New Mexico); to find it, head to the well-known El Taco de Mexico (714 Santa Fe Drive), Brewery Bar II (150 Kalamath Street), Efrain's (with three locations at *efrainsrestaurant.com*), or The Original Chubby's (1231 W. 38th Avenue).

The drinking scene is amazing, of course; not only is Denver one of the country's top craft-beer destinations, with some 100 breweries in the metro area, but it's also got a thriving distillery/cocktail scene.

Some of the most widely acclaimed spots in town for food and/or drinks are Acorn (American cuisine at 3350 Brighton Boulevard; phone: 720.542.3721), Mizuna (more American cuisine at 225 E. 7th Avenue; phone: 303.832.4778), Mercantile (1701 Wynkoop Street, #155; phone: 720.460.3733), Rioja (latin flavors at 1431 Larimer Street; phone: 303.820.2282), Williams & Graham (a prohibition-era speakeasy at 3160 Tejon Street; phone: 303.997.8886), Work & Class (homestyle southern and latin food at 2500 Larimer Street; phone: 303.292.0700), Root Down (a converted filling station serving small plates at 1600 W. 33rd Avenue; phone: 303.993.4200), Beast + Bottle (American cuisine and a boutique bar at 719 E. 17th Avenue; phone: 303.623.3223), Bar Dough (Italian cuisine at 2227 W. 32nd Avenue), Hop Alley (Chinese at 3500 Larimer Street), Old Major (a sustainable spot that describes itself as rustic chic at 3316 Tejon Street; phone: 720.420.0622), and Guard and Grace (a modern steakhouse at 1801 California Street; phone: 303.293. 8500).

In Boulder, Frasca (for Northern Italian food made with locally sourced ingredients at 1738 Pearl Street; phone: 303.442.6966) also deserves its accolades.

That said, my personal favorites at the moment are:

Rebel (3763 Wynkoop Street; phone: 303.297.3902), run by two zany chefs with a highly adventurous menu (think lamb's head platters, fried tripe poutine in foie gras gravy, turnips four ways, etc.);

To the Wind (3333 E. Colfax Avenue; phone: 303.316.3333), which is tiny, with a closet-sized kitchen surrounded by a chef's counter, headed by a delightful husband and wife team, and serving terrific contemporary bistro fare;

The Way Back (4132 W. 38th Avenue; phone: 720.728.8156), a super stylish and fun spot with suave cocktails and small plates like lionfish sashimi;

Beast + Bottle (see above);

Coperta, a killer neo-trattoria with a mozzarella bar and fan-tastic "spuzzulia" (essentially amuse bouche platters);

19

Stoic & Genuine (1701 Wynkoop Street; phone: 303.640.3474), a sexy seafood spot in Union Station doing innovative stuff like octopus mortadella and uni fried rice, as well as classics (lobster rolls, tuna melts). The raw bar is augmented by a granita bar where different flavors of shived ice garnish oysters and cocktails;

And Palenque Mezcaleria (1294 S. Broadway), an atmospheric cocktail bar emphasizing mescal and Oazacan-style nibbles.

Budget Tips
Despite its explosive growth and housing price increases, Denver's still not an expensive town. You can have a field day doing a brewery crawl without spending loads. I'm an international-food nerd and so I love to go to Aurora to eat, where Asian and African restaurants of all kinds are to be found. Of course, Mexican food is everywhere and it's terrific and cheap.

Best Places to Take a Photo
For the Denver skyline, a restaurant with a great rooftop patio like Linger or Avanti is a good idea.

Find Ruth at ruthtobias.com.

THE INTERVIEWS

Amber Johnson
Editor of the Mile High Mamas.

About Amber

I'm Amber Johnson—a born and raised Canadian now living in a Denver suburb. I'm the editor of Mile High Mamas, Colorado's longest-running and most established social media community for moms. In my free time, I enjoy spending time outdoors with my family.

What to do in Denver (the Basics)

One of my family's favorite stops with first-time visitors is Red Rocks Amphitheater, an iconic concert venue that is famous with locals as a great place to run stairs. There are some great hikes in the area, a grill, and gift shop.

We also love the 16th Street Mall, LoDo (lower downtown), and Larimer Square for shopping and restaurants. Union Station was recently revamped and has a fun spray fountain in front, along with The Crawford Hotel and some pretty iconic local restaurants such as The Kitchen, Next Door, and Community Pub.

Hidden Gems for Seasoned Travelers

If you love the outdoors, be sure to stop by REI's flagship store located right on the Platte River. Watch the kayakers navigate the park while splashing around in Confluence Park. And follow the trail a few blocks to Little Man Ice Cream, about the coolest shop around, in the shape of a creamery can.

Day Trips

Hike St. Mary's Glacier, about a 45-minute drive from Denver. This is a short but steep trail that leads to some of the most gorgeous views in the Colorado Rockies. Top off your day with lunch at Beau Jo's Colorado Style Pizza in Idaho Springs (1517 Miner Street).

Another favorite day trip for out-of-towners is to take them to the top of a 14er. Colorado has 54 peaks that are over 14,000 feet, two of which you can drive to the summit. Pikes Peak is about an hour away in Colorado Springs (you can also take a cog train to the top) and we also love driving to Mt. Evans, after which we stop at my favorite breakfast place in Colorado: Country Road Cafe in Kittredge (26490 Highway 74).

Where to Walk
Start at Jeffco Open Space Parks and Trails. Alderfer Three Sisters Park's Summit Trail is a favorite. And when my kids want to cool down, we go to Lair O' the Bear Park where they play in Bear Creek.

Boulder is amazing for hiking as well. Be sure to go to Chautauqua Park and grab a bite to eat after at their historic dining hall, voted best outdoor dining in Colorado.

What & Where to Eat & Drink
The Kitchen (1530 16th Street; phone: 303.623.3127) has amazing small plates in a community-style setting. For a great burger, try Lark Burger (4660 W 121st Avenue #1; phone: 720.452.2410)—their truffle fries are to-die-for!—and The Cherry Cricket (2641 E. 2nd Avenuve; phone: 303.322.7666).

Best Places to Take a Photo
From atop the amphitheater at Red Rocks.

Find Amber at milehighmamas.com.

THE INTERVIEWS

BOULDER
A liberal, artsy university town nestled against the mountains.

FIND WI-FI HERE: Pearl Street Mall (free public Wi-Fi) and The Cup Espresso Bar.

Allan Wright
Foodie. Tour Business Owner.

About Allan
I am originally from Seattle, have lived in four US time zones and three foreign countries, and have planted myself for the last 12 years in Boulder.

I run a small company with three divisions that run food, wine, and beer tours around the world and organize food, drink, and fitness conferences. I also co-founded and manage the multi-contributor website Eat Drink Boulder which covers the food and drink scene in Boulder County.

In my free time, I play soccer twice a week, hike, bike, and run. I also volunteer with a non-profit called Boulder Friends of International Students.

What to do in Boulder (the Basics)
Pearl Street Mall—a four-block section of downtown Boulder closed to cars since 1976—is the center of the city. This simple idea had huge positive effects and the area now hosts loads of restaurants, bars, and shops. Street performers station themselves throughout the mall in the summer months. So start there for a self-guided walking tour.

Families with small kids should visit the Pop Jet Fountain in front of the County Courthouse. Kids love dancing through trying to

23

avoid getting wet and parents love the smiles and shrieks of laughter. Adults can hit the rooftop bars of the Rio (1101 Walnut Street) or Lazy Dog (1346 Pearl Street) restaurants.

For those who need a coffee shop to sneak away and get some work done, I prefer The Cup (1521 Pearl Street), which is always packed in the front room and on the patio, but has a "hidden" back room that works well for meetings.

Hidden Gems for Seasoned Travelers

Get out of Boulder and up into the mountains. There are dozens of outstanding high-altitude mountain paths in western Boulder County. The Fourth of July trailhead just west of Eldora is the start of a dozen trails all by itself and is a great way to get into the high country without a lot of effort. The Brainerd Lake area is another excellent opportunity to get into the Indian Peaks Wilderness with both short and long hiking trails.

The University of Colorado is right next to downtown Boulder but mostly gets missed by the average tourist; it is well worth doing a little advance research to watch a sporting event, listen to a lecture, or catch a play.

Where to Stay

Anything between the mountains to the west and 28th Street to the east north of Baseline Road and south of Alpine Avenue is considered downtown Boulder, which is a nice place to stay.

Your best bet is to be within walking distance of Pearl Street. Outside this area, Boulder is not all that big and the only real neighborhood worth staying in as a visitor is North Boulder, which has become a hip area with restaurants and bars.

For unique lodging, check out the Colorado Chautauqua National Historic Landmark, which rents 58 cottages and has amazing access to the mountains.

THE INTERVIEWS

Day Trips

The single best day trip destination from Boulder is Estes Park. Located less than an hour away, it's a cute small mountain town that is the gateway to Rocky Mountain National Park, the most visited national park in Colorado and one of the best in the country. Visitors can make a loop trip by returning on the Peak to Peak Highway through Nederland (itself a fun small town and considered the bastion of hippyism in the county). Estes Park can get crowded, so it is best to go in shoulder season or on weekdays.

Where to Walk

What makes Boulder truly unique is its commitment to open space. Both the city and county have preservation programs with 45,000 and 103,000 acres of protected land that will never be developed. The City of Boulder alone has over 145 miles of trails. While all are worth exploring, three of note to visitors are:

The Boulder Creek Path: a paved trail perfect for walking or biking;

Mount Sanitas: a nice loop with both an easy section and a difficult section accessible from downtown;

And Chautauqua: a National Historic Landmark with lots of hiking trails and the most popular destination for visitors who wish to hike.

What & Where to Eat & Drink

There is no "Boulder cuisine" per se, but two things stand out here: locally sourced fare and beer. Chefs go way above and beyond creating dishes with local ingredients. Many of the best restaurants have partnerships with local farms or even own farms themselves. Simply ask your server for whatever is local and you will get a long list of dishes.

Boulder is also well known for its craft beer. Yes, much of the country is now swimming in craft beer, but Boulder leads the way. Not only is it home to the national Brewers Assocation trade group and Homebrewers Association membership group but it also boasts the oldest craft brewery in Colorado: Boulder Beer Company, founded in 1979.

The Mediterranean (at 1002 Walnut Street; phone: 303.444. 5335, known as The Med) is an outstanding choice for quality food at reasaonable prices with a fun atmosphere.

The Rio Grande (1101 Walnut Street; phone: 303.444.3690) serves family-friendly Mexican nicely balanced with delicious and powerful margaritas.

The Kitchen (1039 Pearl Street; phone: 303.544.5973) is an up-scale restaurant on the west side of downtown that has two sister restaurants, The Kitchen Upstairs and the Kitchen Next Door, perfect for more casual dining.

Mountain Sun (1535 Pearl Street) is a local brewpub that is always packed, doesn't take credit cards, provides outstanding service, and serves good food and their own beers.

Avery Brewing (4910 Nautilus Court) is famous across the US for its interesting beers. If you have a beer-lover in your group, go here and ask the very knowledgeable staff to recommend a flight of tasters.

Budget Tips

Boulder's downtown restaurant scene is often packed on Thursday, Friday, and Saturday nights, forcing locals to arrive early. But that's fine because most of us don't have 9 - 5 jobs and because almost every restaurant in downtown Boulder has an excellent happy hour that serves the same great food at lower prices. Eating dinner before 6 p.m. is a great way to experience Boulder on a budget.

In terms of activity, most visitors don't spend lots of money since biking, hiking, and walking are the main attractions. Boulder BCycle is a community bike rental system with bike stands throughout the city.

THE INTERVIEWS

How to Fit In

Don't smoke on Pearl Street Mall (or anywhere, for that matter). Not only is it illegal, but locals don't appreciate smoke, be it tobacco or cannabis. Speaking of cannabis, you can find lots of shops to purchase what you like. But the amazing thing about Colorado's new marijuana laws is that it has had almost no effect on our daily lives. We rarely see people smoking and never see any negative consequences of legalization. So be cautious, don't overindulge, and you'll blend in fine.

Also, for the most part, politics is not a subject we discuss much. While everyone cares, we are mostly occupied with other activities. Plus, almost everyone you meet will be some shade of liberal, which works well because we tend more towards intellectual conversation than back-and-forth arguments.

How to Meet Locals & Make Friends

Join a group. There are local groups for everything and you can easily participate in a hike, bike ride, yoga class, environmental meeting, meditation course, or any of a number of 100 other interesting activities. A good place to start is *meetup.com*.

Best Places to Take a Photo

The classic view of Boulder is of the Flatirons, which are the rock formations resembling irons just west of the city.

Final Notes & Other Tips

One of the most interesting aspects of Boulder and, in fact, the entire Front Range is that we are situated in a geologically important area. The hills just to the west of the city are the start of the famous Rocky Mountains. But what people don't really understand is that essentially we are also the start of the Great Plains. Situated at 5,430 feet of elevation, the land gradually slopes downward all the way to the Mississippi River.

Find Allan at eatdrinkboulder.com and zephyradventures.com.

THE INTERVIEWS

FORT COLLINS

A hip university town with a cool brewery scene.

FIND WI-FI HERE: Wild Boar Café, Starry Night Espresso Café, Downtown Artery Café, & Alley Cat Coffee House.

Stacey McKenna
Writer. Climber. Volunteer. Traveler.

About Stacey
I'm 36, originally from the DC suburbs, and moved to Arizona before high school. After college in southern California, I moved around a lot (five states and three non-US countries in seven years) before landing in Fort Collins, where I've been since 2007.

I'm a freelance writer and spend my spare time walking my amazing 10-year-old shelter pup, climbing, reading, volunteering for a racehorse re-homing organization, substitute teaching yoga at the county jail, and generally loving the flexibility of my and my husband's careers by traveling locally and abroad as much as possible. I've also started painting recently (never thought that would happen!).

What to do in Fort Collins (the Basics)
My favorite thing to do with visitors is to fill days with a mix of eating, drinking, biking, and hiking. Usually we just ride bikes (when it's nice out) to old town and hop between cideries, distilleries, breweries, and restaurants.

Must-dos for first-timers are a brewery tour (there are *many* to choose from, but I recommend New Belgium or Odell since they're really our flagship spots). If folks are committed to Budweiser over craft brews or happen to be horse-lovers, a trip to the Budweiser brewery north of town can be interesting, as well.

Athletic types can do a bicycle tour of several of the town's breweries as well (*beerandbiketours.com/tours*), though these I haven't done through a company.

There are loads of nice hiking and biking spots around the city and the Fort Collins Bike Share (*bikefortcollins.org*; bike rentals $10 per day) means you can get around on two wheels without lugging a cycle on the airplane.

As for touristy things to skip? Maybe skip riding the trolley (which is not very functional) and consider taking The Max instead (a new designated-route bus that runs between old town and the southern end of the city).

Hidden Gems for Seasoned Travelers
Swetsville Zoo is *amazing*. A sculptor takes all kinds of farm equipment and creates giant creatures—from dinosaurs to ants—throughout his property. Visitors can wander the grounds and ogle the strangeness. It's very Fort Collins, donation based, and set along the riverbank.

Check out some of the smaller breweries and our growing collection of distilleries and cideries. And Nuance Chocolate (one of only two or three bean-to-bar shops in Colorado).

Fort Collins Museum of Art has some cool exhibits, though I'd just as highly recommend checking out the Downtown Artery Gallery or just looking for art on the walls of restaurants and bars (many of which exhibit local artists' works). Global Village Museum can also have some neat cultural exhibits for folks who are so inclined, and the Fort Collins Museum of Discovery and The Farm at Lee Martinez Park are good for kids.

Where to Stay
Old Town will give you the best access to things, especially if you don't want to deal with driving. The Downtown Artery has

an Airbnb listing (though it may be limited to bands performing there, so check before you plan to book).

For folks with a vehicle, the city is small enough that you can get away with staying wherever. My mom and stepdad always stay at a KOA north of town. My dad used to stay at a hotel in mid-town and the bulk of hotels are on the south end, though that's also where it'll be harder to find local businesses. There are also a couple of B&Bs on Mountain Avenue that would give good access to old town.

The hotels on East Mulberry and North College streets tend to not be the most savory and I wouldn't recommend either of these areas to tourists. Folks wanting more of a country feel could check out the town of Laporte just outside Fort Collins' city limits but still only a 15-minute drive from old town (probably closer than the south end, actually).

Day Trips

For a super close escape, try Estes Park, a cute tourist town with loads of accommodations and the gateway to Rocky Mountain National Park. Poudre Canyon is another great option, with some nice hiking and camping options as well as The Mishawaka (13714 Poudre Canyon Road, Bellvue, Colorado), a fun riverside restaurant/bar/music venue. It's a great place to stop for an afternoon beer after a morning hike or to go for a concert. And it's a pretty drive when the leaves are changing.

For folks willing to go a bit further afield, there are some great mountain escapes with hot springs (which is my favorite kind of mountain getaway). Steamboat is about 3.5 hours away and is fantastic! It's a small ski town with excellent food and magical hot springs (Strawberry Park Hot Springs). Glenwood Springs is about four hours away and is another fun mountain getaway-type spot with one of my favorite ever farm-to-table restaurants (The Pullman; 330 7th Street; 970.230.9234) and more developed but gigantic hot springs. If the weather's good, people can get to Saratoga, Wyoming, which is about 2.5 hours away and has some stunning camping around it (Bennett Peak Campground) as well as hot springs and fishing galore in the very small town.

Where to Walk

City Park is a great spot for taking a walk, having a picnic, playing frisbee, etc. There's a playground, sports courts/fields, and a small lake. This is definitely a local park and is busy year-round.

Spring Creek Trail and the Poudre River Trail Corridor are both beautiful spots that run through town east-west and make for nice biking/walking/running trails along rivers.

The town butts up to the foothills, so there are loads of hiking options there. I like the Reservoir Ridge trails or the loop around Dixon Reservoir at Pineridge Natural Area. Both of these areas see loads of mountain bikers, too.

And walking around old town is always pleasant (apparently, Walt Disney modeled Disneyland's Main Street and many of its buildings after old town).

What & Where to Eat & Drink

We've been called the Napa Valley of beer, so I definitely recommend folks indulge while here. There's really something craft for everybody; at last count, I think we had at least 14 breweries, though I can't really keep track.

I can't drink beer because of gluten sensitivity, but when I did, my favorite was Odell (800 E. Lincoln Avenue). New Belgium (500 Linden Street) is popular and the brewery has loads of character. Both of these are on the outskirts of old town.

Other popular spots in and around old town include Equinox (133 Remington Street), Horse & Dragon (124 Racquette Drive), which is fairly new but probably a local favorite right now, and Fort Collins Brewery and Tavern (1020 E. Lincoln Avenue), which has a pretty good restaurant, but awful service. I've heard mixed reviews of Pateros Creek (242 N. College Avenue), but

31

personally love them for having seriously delicious gluten-free beers.

We also now have a cidery that I love, which also serves food. Scrumpy's (215 N. College Avenue) serves casual sandwich-type fare. They've recently expanded and have a couple of fun flight options.

Feisty Spirits Distillery (1708 E. Lincoln Avenue #1) is a distillery on the outskirts of town. They make mostly whiskeys and use an assortment of unique grains. They do some cocktails and tours. CopperMuse Distillery (244 N. College Avenue) is in old town. They mostly make vodkas and rums, I think, but they also have craft cocktails and a fun food menu. And a new distillery—Elevation 5003 (2601 S. Lemay Avenue #8)—just opened, though I haven't been yet.

As for restaurants...I've been told we have more restaurants per-capita than NYC, but my five personal favorites are:

Rainbow Restaurant (212 W. Laurel Street; phone: 970.221.2664) for an awesome veggie-friendly brunch;

Little Bird Café (11 Old Town Square) for delicious coffee and lovely food;

Tasty Harmony (160 W. Oak Street; phone: 970.689.3234) for a mostly vegan menu—my personal favorite lunch/dinner spot in town;

Restaurant 415 (415 S. Mason Street; phone: 970.407.0415), which is an especially fun spot for a group lunch or dinner since you can order more of the menu offerings and share;

And Fish Restaurant & Market (150 W. Oak Street; phone: 970. 224.1188) for responsibly sourced food, casual atmosphere, and exceptional, creative seafood dishes.

Then there's the Waffle Lab—a food truck serving savory and sweet waffles, including gluten-free options. I would put this at the top of my lunch spots list, but the truck can be tricky to find open. If you can find it, though, check it out. Also, they're slated to open their storefront in 2016 at 22 N. College Avenue; phone: 970.690.1888).

If none of those strike your fancy, other good options include:

La Creperie (2722 S. College Avenue), which is just what it sounds like;

La Luz (200 Walnut Street; phone: 970.493.1129) for fish tacos;

Big Al's (140 W. Mountain Avenue; phone: 970.232.9815) for burgers and rotating local art;

Big City Burrito (510 S. College Avenue; phone: 970.482.3303) for wraps that inspire lines out the door;

The Farmhouse at Jessup Farm (1957 Jessup Drive; phone: 970.631.8041)—a new farm-to-table place in an old farmhouse with their own garden and chickens on site (I haven't been yet but have heard only good and plan to go soon);

Café Vino (1200 S. College Avenue; phone: 970.212.3399) for small plates and an excellent wine list;

The Welsh Rabbit Bistro (200 Walnut Street, Unit B; phone: 970.232.9521) for a simple menu centered around artisan cheeses and meats;

As for bars (most of which serve some food and all of which serve local beers), I like:

Social (1 Old Town Square #7), a speakeasy-style spot with craft cocktails and a short but great appetizer menu;

The Town Pump (124 N. College Avenue; phone: 970.493.4404)—a tiny drive-in business since 1909;

THE INTERVIEWS

William Oliver's Publick House (2608 S. Timberline Road) for whiskey flights, cocktails, and a good menu;

The Crown Pub (134 S. College Avenue)—an old standby with good cocktails, a solid menu, and outdoor seating;

And Ace Gillett's Lounge (239 S. College Avenue)—another speakeasy with excellent cocktails, a good menu, and live music.

Budget Tips
Breweries are an affordable (and sometimes free) way to try local beers before hitting the bars. Rent a bike from the FC Bike Library in summer. It'll open the town up to you and it's only $10 a day. If you don't want to spend the money on a museum, lots of restaurants and bars feature local artists—take advantage! We have a lot of great happy hours. Swetsville Zoo is free, as is the local hiking.

How to Fit In
Definitely remember to respect and watch for the bikes. In summer, they swarm and I haven't lived a day in this town without seeing someone on a bicycle. So, especially if you're in a car, watch out for folks on two wheels!

How to Meet Locals & Make Friends
Join some sort of outdoor fitness meetup. People tend to live here for the quality of life and, in this case, that usually involves getting outside and appreciating our amazing location and pretty damn sweet weather.

Best Places to Take a Photo
Try Horsetooth Rock (a five-mile roundtrip hike) or any spot at Swetsville Zoo.

Final Notes & Other Tips
Fort Collins is funny because I can't really distinguish between what a tourist would do and what a local would do. We have lots of great amenities that locals use and tourists would find

attractive, but it doesn't feel like a tourist town to me. Places are here because of the locals. There's huge community investment and a sense that people move here because they want to live a certain way. Life tends to be slow...take your time, be patient, enjoy.

Another key thing: We have all kinds of local. Local beverages, local businesses, locally sourced ingredients, local famers, etc. It's easy to consume locally when here, and it's a pleasure to do so.

Find Stacey at staceymckennawrites.com.

STEAMBOAT SPRINGS
A musical ski town in the Colorado Rockies.

FIND WI-FI HERE: Mountain Brew on Oak Street.

Elissa Greene
Music Festival Organizer. Musician.

About Elissa

I grew up in Wisconsin and Texas, went to college in Colorado Springs, and then moved to Steamboat Springs in 2004. I've been here ever since.

I'm the Executive Director of Strings Music Festival. We present over 60 performances each year of classical music, jazz, rock, country, bluegrass, and other genres, both in the summer and throughout the winter season.

In my free time, I maintain a very small Suzuki cello studio. For fun, I enjoy road cycling in the summer, snowshoeing in the winter, and CrossFit any time of year! I have lived in Steamboat for 12 years, and I just started learning how to ski.

What to do in Steamboat (the Basics)

The Strawberry Park Hot Springs cannot be missed. It is a beautiful spot any time of year and nights are clothing optional. In the summer, Fish Creek Falls is a must-do hike. It's absolutely gorgeous. Tubing down the Yampa River is also a great time.

In colder weather, check out the many winter activities offered by the Steamboat Ski Resort, as well as snowshoeing and cross-country skiing around the valley.

Hidden Gems for Seasoned Travelers

The small towns of Clark and Oak Creek, both less than 45-minutes from Steamboat, are throwbacks to the early days of settlement in northwest Colorado. Steamboat Lake in North Routt County (near Clark) is a beautiful lake surrounded by majestic mountains. Stagecoach Reservoir is in South Routt County (near Oak Creek) and also offers a fun time. Just north of the reservoir is the Sarvis Creek Wilderness Area; there are great hikes and fishing around this area. It's gorgeous!

Where to Stay

The great thing about Steamboat is the proximity of the ski resort to the town, a thing that isn't always common in ski towns. Historic downtown Steamboat Springs is a great place to stay, but there aren't as many lodging options as there are on the mountain. There are hotels, condos, townhomes, rental vacation homes...something for everyone.

Day Trips

There is so much to see in the small area of Steamboat, but it's not too far to venture to Clark and Stagecoach (see above).

Where to Walk

Steamboat has a fantastic 7.5-mile paved trail called the Yampa River Core Trail that runs along the Yampa River. You can walk, bike, rollerblade, jog with your dog, or use it as a means of transportation through downtown. You can enter the Yampa River Botanic Park from the trail, as well.

What & Where to Eat & Drink

While in the west, experience what we are known for: great meat! We have fantastic ranches in the area. Check out Sweetwood Cattle Company for high-quality beef and Elkstone Farm for produce and other great products. Many local restaurants feature Yampa Valley beef and lamb and Elkstone products on their menus.

My favorite restaurant in Steamboat is Café Diva (1855 Ski Time Square Drive; phone: 970.871.0508). It's great for a special occasion or a romantic evening. It is a little pricey but worth

THE INTERVIEWS

every penny. Both the service and the food are the best in town. Call ahead for reservations; they fill up quickly

Other favorites are Carl's Tavern (700 Yampa Street) for American fare, Salt & Lime (628 Lincoln Avenue) for Mexican street-style food, and Noodles & More (635 Lincoln Avenue) for Vietnamese food and sushi. Noodles & More is always busy with locals, but is definitely off the radar for tourists!

Budget Tips
Noodles & More is budget-friendly. Sunpie's Bistro (735 Yampa Avenue) is another budget-friendly restaurant/bar.

The Core Trail is free to use and is fun for the whole family. Tubing down the Yampa River is reasonable: buy your own tube or visit Backdoor Sports on 9th and Yampa for daily tube rentals, which also includes a shuttle to put in further up the river.

Finally, for winter activities, book early! The ski resort offers discounts on most of their products if you purchase at least seven days in advance.

How to Fit In
Either learn how to drive in the snow (Steamboat gets 400+ inches of snow each year!) or leave the driving to the professionals. There are plenty of taxis and shuttles to get you where you need to go without renting a car and risking your life and the lives of those around you.

Also, be nice to service industry workers! These folks want you to have a good experience in our community and will do their best to give you that. However, it's not very affordable to live in a ski town and many people have two or three jobs. Tip well.

How to Meet Locals & Make Friends
When you're skiing, ride the lift and strike up a conversation with folks around you...you'll probably make a new friend!

Best Places to Take a Photo

Sunset Happy Hour at the top of the ski mountain takes place Thursday evenings in the summer and winter. It costs $12 and includes the gondola ride and $5 off your first drink. The views are spectacular!

Also, hike up Emerald Mountain to the top of the ski jump on Howelsen Hill: this provides a great view of downtown!

Find Elissa at stringsmusicfestival.com.

COLORADO SPRINGS
Food and old west charm nestled against the mountains.

FIND WI-FI HERE: Maté Factor Café.

Jacqueline Perez
Chef. Hiker. Musician.

About Jacqueline

I was born in San Jose, California, and moved to Colorado Springs when I was three years old. There's a popular bumper sticker in Colorado that says "Native" with mountains in the background; when that became popular, an alternative sticker was created that says "not a native, but I got here as soon as I could". I guess you can say I got here as soon as I could. And like many, I have Colorado pride.

I currently live in Manitou Springs, which is 15 minutes west of Colorado Springs. My mom and I own and run a Mexican restaurant, though we're now in the transition of selling it. When I'm not working, I'm hanging out with friends at breweries, hiking, or playing at a jam session.

What to do in Colorado Springs (the Basics)

Garden of the Gods is a *must see*. The rock formations can be seen from your car or on foot while hiking easy family-friendly trails.

The Air Force base, on the other hand, is on my "not worth it" list. It takes most of the day to get a permit get on base. They also have strict traffic rules. It is more of hassle than anything. A cool (and better) way to see the base is off the 1-25 pull offs.

Downtown Colorado Springs is another must. It has great eats. The Kimball theater has rare independent films that aren't shown at other theaters. The hotels are great. And the art center right next to Colorado College has some pretty interesting shows for reasonable prices.

Old Colorado City—a five-minute drive from downtown—with its beautiful historical buildings and homes is, in my opinion, the best place to buy all things Colorado (hats, shirts, key chains, all reasonably priced). It also has some one the best live music and karaoke spots in the springs (karaoke typically goes on between Wednesdays and Sundays).

And, of course, Manitou Springs is a must see. This town is located in a canyon at the foot of Pikes Peak (another must-see). The main road that goes through Garden of the Gods (yet another must-see) leads straight to Manitou Springs. And, conveniently, all these must-see spots are near each other.

Hidden Gems for Seasoned Travelers

Colorado has some of the most breathtaking hikes and outdoor scenery I have experienced. For more adventurous travelers, some of my must-see hiking and scenery spots are:

Seven Falls/Helen Hunt Falls. This hike can vary from easy to intermediate. If you stay on the Helen Hunt Falls Trail, its an easy 20-minute walk. Hikes around the area, such as Mt. Cutler can give you a bit more of a workout and challenge.

Cave of the Winds is every geologist's dream. These caves contain unique minerals and have tours open to the public. Pro tip: If you are afraid of small, tight areas, the tour might be a bit difficult.

Red Rock Canyon is located on the west side of Colorado Springs, off Highway 24. This hiking trail is special in that back in the early 1900s, Colorado miners mined through these rocks leaving interesting formations. There are also dinosaur footprints that can be found in the rocks.

Back in town, The Broadmore is a beautiful neighborhood with a high-class hotel that is worth seeing and the Cheyenne Mountain Zoo is a gem.

Where to Stay

I recommend the north or west sides of the city. The north side has a nice outlet, a few nice hiking areas (Ute Valley Park and Mount Blodgett). The north side is also closer to Castlerock and Denver, if you want to visit those places. The west side, on the other hand, has some of my favorite eats, bars, and hiking spots. There are a few hikes out there that make you feel like you are truly away from civilization. This side of town can get backed up with traffic, but there's a nice straightaway from Manitou Springs to Old Colorado all the way to downtown.

Day Trips

Woodland Park is about a 40-minute car trip and in the fall season the drive is incredible. In the winter, it's a beautiful winter wonderland. In the summer, there are many fun campsites (I suggest Crags Campground if you're on a budget; it's free, beautiful, and safe!).

Denver is only an hour away. It has the home stadium of the super-winning NFL team, the Broncos, as well as tons of great music venues.

Where to Walk

Check out the suggestions above and the Sante Fe Trail, which is one of the oldest trails in Colorado (if not *the* oldest). It was used as a trading road for the pioneers. The trail goes all the way through New Mexico.

What & Where to Eat & Drink

Food is one of the dearest things to me. I am actually a chef and have worked in quite a few kitchens in this town. One thing to know about Colorado is that we love things to be local. We like our vegetables and meat and especially beer to be all local. The restaurants that have these qualities really win our community over.

Maté Factor Café (966 Manitou Ave in Manitou Springs) is a unique cafe that sells a healing and energizing tea called maté. Its definitely worth checking out.

My absolute favorite places to eat and drink around town are: Shugas (702 S. Cascade Avenue; phone: 719.328.1412) for its coconut shrimp soup and the "beet down," a delicious beet-infused vodka drink;

Poor Richards (320 N. Tejon Street), where you can build your own pizza;

Coquette's Bistro & Bakery (321 N. Tejon Street; phone: 719.685.2420) for gluten-free cupcakes;

Burrowing Owl (1791 S. 8th Street; phone: 719.434.3864) for vegan taco salad and a drink called "The Watermelon Situation," which features whiskey and fresh watermelon;

Brother Luck Street Eats (1005 W. Colorado Avenue; phone: 719.434.2741) for Cuban sandwiches and peach tea;

La Baguette (2417 W. Colorado Avenue; phone: 719.577.4818) for baked goods;

Front Range (2330 W. Colorado Avenue; phone: 719.632.2596) for its chicken BBQ plate;

Red Leg Brewing Company (4630 Forge Road) for a Devil Dog Stout;

And 15C Club Martini & Cigar Bar (15 E. Bijou Street) for a dirty martini.

Budget Tips
Some of our dive bars are my favorite places to go in town. Check out Benny's, Mill Hill Saloon, Tony's, and Royal Tavern. Or just look up happy hours; we have a ton.

THE INTERVIEWS

How to Fit In

Please don't assume every local is a pot smoker. Religion is a touchy subject in Colorado Springs...Christianity being a main one. And we are proud of our local beer so if you don't like it...get out! (Kidding. Sort of.)

How to Meet Locals & Make Friends

Check out the bars, festivals, shows, and community work opportunities.

MANITOU SPRINGS

A quirky mountain town at the foot of Pike's Peak.

FIND WI-FI HERE: Manitou Community Library, Good Karma, The Loft Coffee Shop, and Mate Factor Cafe.

Leah Fenimore
Pianist. Hiker. Entrepreneur.

About Leah

I am originally from Littleton, just over an hour from Manitou. I work with Cave of the Winds as well as the Pikes Peak Library District. In my free time, I play piano, hike, work on my business, exercise, and play with my dog.

What to do in Manitou Springs (the Basics)

Definitely check out all the beautiful trails in the area (except the incline, which is extraordinarily busy, especially on weekends, with people everywhere and many of them rude).

The outdoor rides at Cave of the Winds (a 500-million-year-old cave) are a blast. And the other fun thing to do is take a tour of all the drinkable mineral springs in town. You can get a map of them all online (*manitoumineralsprings.org*) or at the Visitor's Bureau in town. They are what Manitou is famous for.

I would not recommend the cliff dwellings, which are not native to this area and seem to have been transplanted from somewhere else.

Hidden Gems for Seasoned Travelers

The Midland Railroad Tunnels (a trail that leads through a series of old train tunnels) is a favorite, as is the Cameron Cone Hike.

45

THE INTERVIEWS

Ute Pass Trail also is a very nice stroll above the town of Cascade.

Where to Stay
Manitou Springs is so small that you could stay anywhere and get a feel for the city, except for maybe up in Crystal Park area.

Day Trips
I recommend going on a hike in Cheyenne Cañon Park or driving into Cripple Creek for some gambling and learning about the old gold mining industry. Victor (an old abandoned mining town with gorgeous views and great hikes), Woodland Park (for more hiking), Cascade (for more hiking that's less congested than the Manitou trails), and Cañon City (for the Royal Gorge) are all also close by and interesting to visit.

Where to Walk
Check out the Ute Pass Trail (mentioned above), Red Mountain Trail, and Intemann Trail for hiking.

The best park in Manitou is Memorial Park. It's got a great playground and is across the street from both a wonderful spa and Seven Minute Springs, which I recommend taking a drink from!

What & Where to Eat & Drink
Adam's Mountain Café (26 Manitou Avenue) is a *must* for a lunch date. It's a bit on the pricey side, but the food is beyond amazing. They have something for every taste. Try their vegan vanilla cashew cake!

Other great places to check out are Good Karma coffee shop (110 Canon Avenue), Swirl Wine Bar (717 Manitou Avenue, #102) for delicious wines and their Wednesday night trivia, Manitou Brewing Company (725 Manitou Avenue), which has delicious food and great local beers, Adam's Mountain Café (for amazing vegan fare and sustainable meals), Townhouse Lounge (for karaoke), and Sahara Café (for great, affordable falafel gyros and stuffed grape leaves).

46

Budget Tips

The tourist attractions are expensive. Go easy on those. Hiking is free. And, depending on the trail, there are educational signposts along the way where you can learn about the history of the trail, also for free.

How to Fit In

Don't drive up Ruxton Avenue. Take the free shuttle instead. It's much easier, you won't have parking hassles, and you won't annoy the natives who are probably trying to get to work.

How to Meet Locals & Make Friends

There are always locals hanging out and playing music on the sidewalks in the main part of town. It's also very common to meet people on trails or at the music or triva events later at night at the bars.

Best Places to Take a Photo

Anywhere up any of the hiking trails. Or anywhere along the road or at the top parking lot of Cave of the Winds.

CAÑON CITY

A quiet cowboy town with a famous train.

FIND WI-FI HERE: The library, McDonald's, and Coyote Coffee Den in nearby Penrose.

Bobbi & Don Taylor
Horse Lovers. Live Music Afficionados. Entrepreneurs.

About Bobbi & Don

Don and I retired from our respective companies in 1999 and made our first move to Colorado to begin a life of retirement, travel, and fun. We started in Breckenridge and built our dream log home, only to get restless, needing a project where both of us could learn something new together.

We chose the horse business and began our journey of training, buying, selling, showing, and riding Peruvian horses. We then moved from Breck and built an equestrian paradise in the small town of Guffey.

Fast forward to 2008: once again feeling the need for something new (and better weather), we built another ranch in Cañon City, where we reside today.

We have five horses and spend our time traveling, exploring this beautiful state on horseback, playing golf, going to music festivals, doing home projects, gardening, and wintering in Palm Springs, California.

What to do in Cañon City (the Basics)

Cañon City is best known for the Royal Gorge, which boasts the highest suspension bridge in the US and gets as many visitors per year as the Grand Canyon. You can cross the bridge and the park from up top, ride the Royal Gorge Route Railroad through the bottom of the gorge, and/or whitewater raft your way down the gorge. Our favorite rafting company is Raft Masters (*raftmasters.com*). We now also have many zip lines to enhance the Royal Gorge experience. The Cloudscraper by ZipRider is the highest zipline in North America.

There are also, new to the town, some scenic Jeep tours (*coloradojeeptours.com*), so if you want to see the area but don't want to hike, bike, or ride, that's another option. Or you can "play dirty" on an ATV tour (*playdirtyatvtours.com*).

Fishing is abundant in the area, especially all along the Arkansas River. The brown trout population in this river is second to none.

We also have a winery that is housed in the old abbey (at 3011 E. Highway 50) and it's very interesting, though I am not a personal fan of their wines.

Hidden Gems for Seasoned Travelers
Royal Gorge Helitours—a helicopter touring company—is a special treat. Take a ride over the gorge and surrounding area. It surprises people that such a small town has something like this, but we do. I highly recommend this one.

Another hidden gem is our Fourmile Ranch Golf Club. It's a great course with a desert feel, lots of elevation changes, and some blind holes designed by the talented Jim Engh.

In June, July, August, and September, we have live jazz on the lawn at the library on the first Friday of the month. It's free and the shops downtown stay open late and often serve food/ drinks or have music. It's a lively time to be downtown.

Where to Stay
The best place in town is a B&B called the Jewel of the Canyons. There are also a few Airbnb and VRBO houses and we have a few decent RV parks with full hookups.

49

Day Trips

Experience the magic of a real pioneer town in the nearby town of Florence, a renowned destination for antiques, art, gifts, and eateries, and, my personal favorite: an adorable, tasty bakery called Aspen Leaf Bakery & Cafe (113 W. Main Street), perfect for a nice lunch.

Cripple Creek is another gem: an old mining town nearby, it's a great historical retreat and the home of many casinos and restaurants. Check out the Mollie Kathleen Gold Mine, the Homestead House Museum (an 1890s brothel), and the Cripple Creek and Victor Narrow Gauge railroad. There are also many historical venues/homes that have been converted to B&Bs. Our personal favorite is the Carr Manor House, a converted old schoolhouse. Our favorite restaurant in town is Bronco Billy's Steakhouse in the Bronco Billy Casino (phone: 719.689.2909).

Plus, there is the Scenic Gold Belt Byway Phantom Canyon Road/Shelf Road—a dirt road that goes from Canon City to Cripple Creek that can create an adventure in itself with tremendous views. Keep in mind that it's not for the faint of heart—especially those with a fear of heights—as the road is narrow and high in many spots. And Cripple Creek is also reachable by a normal road in another direction.

Breckenridge is only an hour and a half one way and that is a delightful town in summer and winter.

The drive to nearby Salida along the Arkansas River is beautiful and Salida has been called the "little Aspen" of southcentral Colorado. It is a funky artist town filled with resale and antique shops, art galleries, restaurants, and many festivals each year.

Colorado Springs is the home of Pikes Peak, which you can either drive up to or take the cog rail out of Manitou Springs to get up. The Broadmoor Hotel—the only five-star hotel in Colorado—is also in Colorado Springs. The Airforce Academy and Olympic Training Center are there too. And the town has a vibrant downtown with lots of great nightlife and music.

Nearby, Manitou Springs has lots of shopping and restaurants, plus many charming B&Bs. Old Colorado City is also in the neighborhood, with lots of shops and restaurants all unique to the area. And don't miss Garden of the Gods for hiking, biking, and horseback riding through the natural splendor of the rock formations.

Where to Walk

Right in the heart of downtown is the River Walk, a beautiful 12-mile trail that goes along the river and then up on some high vistas for wonderful views of parts of the canyon. You can hike or bike this one.

Also downtown is Skyline Drive—a road with a beautiful view of the entire city.

North of town, you'll find lots of hiking and mountain biking at the Oil Wells Flats and the trails connected to the Sand Gulch Campgrounds and The Bank Campgrounds. You can hike into a wonderful canyon. The area also boasts world-class rock climbing.

What & Where to Eat & Drink

Food is really not the town's specialty. Our one fine dining spot is Le Petit Chablis (512 Royal Gorge Boulevard; phone: 719.269. 3333), a good french restaurant on Highway 50 that is in a cute old house. They also have a French bakery coffee shop right next door for a quick breakfast, snack, or casual lunch.

The best casual restaurant in town is Pizza Madness (509 Main Street; phone: 719.276.3088).

For finer dining, you'll need to venture to DJ's Steakhouse in Pueblo (4289 N. Elizabeth Street; phone: 719.545.9354) or The Famous in Colorado Springs (31 N. Tejon Street; phone: 719.227. 7333), which features live piano music nightly.

One of the rafting companies, Royal Gorge Rafting, has a fun outdoor dining experience complete with volleyball, live music, and a lively scene, but the food is pretty basic (burgers and beer). The place is called White Water Bar & Grill (45045 Highway 50).

Budget Tips

Cañon City is pretty reasonable on all counts and you don't need tons of money to stay, eat, or enjoy, especially as many outdoor activities are free (hiking, biking, rock climbing). If you check the local Shopper paper that comes out on Tuesday, they often have coupons for the attractions (as does the Chamber of Commerce). And now there's a website (*royal gorgetravel.com*) that offers deals and coupons.

How to Fit In

Come ready for a culture of good old western cowboys where everything is super casual and laid back.

How to Meet Locals & Make Friends

Meeting locals is pretty simple. Strike up a conversation with anyone in a retail shop, restaurant, on the train, etc. and you will find people are willing to chat and get to know you. I met my best friend at the local gym.

Best Places to Take a Photo

The most memorable photos are of the Royal Gorge Park, whitewater rafting, or taking the train...or perhaps up high on Skyline Drive or at the top of Pikes Peak in Colorado Springs.

ABOUT THE AUTHOR

Gigi Griffis is a world-traveling entrepreneur and writer with a special love for inspiring stories, new places, and living in the moment. In May 2012, she sold her stuff and took to the road full-time with her freelance business and her pint-sized pooch, Luna.

This year, she's road tripping across the US and Canada, exploring Vancouver, and then heading to the Meditteranean for a winter vacation in Sicily with her partner, Chad.

Gigi is the author of 10 books, including 100 Locals travel guides for Italy, Paris, Prague, Barcelona, Switzerland, France, New York City, Phoenix & Tucson, and, now, the Denver area.

Love what you read here? Find more at *gigigriffis.com*.

ACKNOWLEDGEMENTS

This is the part where I say thank you.

Thank you to all the interviewees, without whom this book (obviously) would not be possible, especially my aunt, Bobbi Taylor, who not only provided a wonderful interview for the book, but has been endlessly supportive of all my book writing efforts over the years.

Thank you to Chad, who has to listen to both my frantic excitement and panicked pre-launch complaints every time I publish one of these.

Thanks to Luna, who is a dog and can't read this, but who makes my life and travels better and frequently leads me to new experiences and interesting people.

And thank you, thank you, thank you to YOU. All my readers. You guys make this all possible.

GOING TRAVELING?

More 100 Locals books are available at gigigriffis.com:

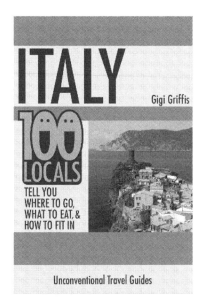

50710833R00033

Made in the USA
Columbia, SC
10 February 2019